How Many on the Log?

by
Sydnie Meltzer Kleinhenz
•
illustrated by
Diane Blasius

Scott Foresman

Editorial Offices: Glenview, Illinois • New York, New York
Sales Offices: Reading, Massachusetts • Duluth, Georgia
Glenview, Illinois • Carrollton, Texas • Menlo Park, California

How many on the log?

One frog on the log.

How many on the log?

Two frogs on the log.

How many on the log?

Three frogs on the log.

How many on the log?

Four frogs on the log.

How many on the log?

Five frogs on the log.

How many on the log?

Six frogs on the log.

How many on the log?

One cat on the log!